Thessaloniki

Text: *Apostolos Papagiannopoulos*
Translation: *A. Pantazidou*
Lay out: *Dot & Color, Spyros Stekoulis*
Photographs: *Apostolos Papagiannopoulos, Rekos, S. Chaidemenos*
Colour separation: *Raster One, Dimitriss Tsatsis*
Makedoniki Chromanalisi

ISBN: 960-7167-66-x

Ⓟ REKOS Ltd.
7 Km Oreokastro st., Tel: (031) 696.587, Fax: (031) 697. 685

←
The White Tower

Leoforos Nikis street in Thessaloniki

The Prefecture of Thessaloniki: Facts and Figures

The Prefecture of Thessaloniki is one of 16 that comprise Northern Greece (Macedonia and Thrace). Thessaloniki together with the prefectures of Imathia, Kilkis, Pella, Pieria and Chalkidiki constitute the area of Central Macedonia.

The prefecture of Thessaloniki covers an area of 3.560 km² and its population (according to the 1991 census) is 946,864 as opposed to 858,661 in the previous census of 1981.

The prefecture of Thessaloniki is divided administratively into two districts: the district of Thessaloniki, with Thessaloniki as its capital, and the district of Langadas, with Langadas as its capital.

The land in the prefecture of Thessaloniki is mainly flat. A huge alluvial plain has been created by the rivers Axios, Gallikos, and Loudias (bordering the prefecture of Pella). To the north, and among the mountains of Vertiskos, Kerdylia, and Chortiatis, a basin has been formed in the district of Langadas by the lakes Aghios Vasilios (or Langadas Lake) and Volvi. Here, the small river Rihios flows into the bay of Strymonikos.

Financially, the prefecture of Thessaloniki is one of the country's most developed areas and contains the greatest concentration of modern industrial units, second only to that of the capital.

The majority of the prefecture's population live within the limits of the city of Thessaloniki. The city's port is one of the main ports in south-east Europe and the largest Greek exports sea outlet.

It has considerably developed agriculture, stock-breeding, and poultry-breeding. It produces: cereals, grains, nuts, animal-feed, vegetables, fruit, olive oil, meat, dairy products, honey, wax, leather, etc.

The main cities in the prefecture of Thessaloniki are: Thessaloniki (pop. 763,173),

The port of Thessaloniki

Langadas (pop. 6,113), Sohos (pop. 3,423), and Koufalia (pop. 7,558).

The main communities in the Greater District of Thessaloniki are: Aghios Athanasios, Aghios Antonios, Adendron, Anatolikon, Aghia Triada, Agelochori, Asvestochori, Chalkidon, Chortiatis, Gefyra, Drymos, Exohi, Epanomi, Kalohori, Kymina, Lagina, Liti, Melissochori, Mikro Monastiri, Nea Mesimvria, Nea Michaniona, Neochorouda, Neo Rysio, Neoi Epivates, Nea Malgara, Oreokastro, Pentalofos, Perea, Plagiari, Prohoma, Philyro, Thermi, Trilofos, Vasilika, Vathilakos.

The main communities in the district of Langadas are: Aghios Vasilios, Arethousa, Askos, Asprovalta, Assiros, Gerakarou, Kavallari, Kolhiko, Krithia, Kryoneri, Nea Apollonia, Nea Madytos, Prophitis, Philladelphion, Stavros, Volvi, Vrasna, Xylopolis, Zangliveri (communities above 1,000 inhabitants each according to the 1991 census).

→
Panoramic view of Thessaloniki

The customs building at the port of Thessaloniki

The statue of Eleftherios Venizelos on Egnatia street

The City of Thessaloniki: Facts and Figures

Thessaloniki is the second largest metropolitan city in the country, after Athens. It is the main centre of development in Northern Greece, and of international fame and appeal.

The city covers an area of 61 km² (6,110 Ha) and has a population of 763,173 according to the census of 1991. This is distributed among its municipalities as follows: Thessaloniki (383,967), Kalamaria (80,698), Ambelokipi (40,093), Stavroupolis (37,596), Sykies (36,347), Neapolis (30,568), Evosmos (28,821), Polihni (27,894), Pylea (20,785), Eleftheriou-Kordelio (16,549), Menemeni (12,932), Triandria (11,822), Nea Ionia (8,127), Panorama (10,275), Aghios Pavlos (7,221), Thermi (7,998), and the Community of Nea Efkarpia (3,480).

Administratively, the city of Thessaloniki is the seat of the Ministry of Macedonia-Thrace, of the District of Central Macedonia, and of the Prefecture of Thessaloniki.

Owing to its active and rapid development, Thessaloniki exerts a direct influence over an area well beyond its actual boundaries. This area is known as the "Greater District of Thessaloniki".

The suburbs of Thessaloniki are: To the north-east - Oreaokastro, Galini, Filiro, Redziki, Asvestohori, Exohi, Chortiatis, and Panorama. To the north-west – Kalohori, Nea Ionia, Halastra (Pyrgos), and Syndos. To the south-east – Thermi, Nea Redestos, Perea, Neoi Epivates, Aghia Triada, Mihaniona, and Epanomi.

The YMCA square in Thessaloniki

→

The old fountain at Syntrivani square

The people of Thessaloniki spend their summer holidays on the beaches of Perea, Neoi Epivates, Aghia Triada, Mihaniona, Epanomi, Chalkidiki, and the gulf of Strimonikos (Asprovalta, Vrasna, Stavros) as well as on the beaches in the prefecture of Pieria (Makrigialos, Methoni, Litohoro, and Leptokaria). The mountainous villages of Pieria, Vermio, Paiko, Vertiskos, Cholomon, and

The Sailing Club

Olympus are ideal for winter holidays. Ski resorts such as "Seli" in Veria, "Tria Pigadia" in Naousa, "Pisoderi" in Florina and "Lalias" in Serres are a major attraction.

Thessaloniki has a "Mediterranean" climate. In winter, the prevailing winds are from the north with a frequency of 18.9% as compared to a frequency of 9.8% from the east. The most characteristic wind is the "famous" Vardaris which blows down the valley of Axios and keeps pollution at bay. In summer the prevailing winds are from the south (9.3%) and from the south-west (10.5%).

Maximum monthly rainfall is 189.3 mm, while the average rainfall for August is 14.2 mm, for July it is 22.6 mm, and for December it is 55.2 mm.

The air temperature makes the climate of Thessaloniki more continental than that of other west Mediterranean areas. The maximum temperatures are observed in July (+41.8° C) while

The marina at Kalamaria

the minimum in January (-10.3° C).

Average relative humidity during July and August is 60%, while at times it may reach as low as 30%.

Thessaloniki enjoys 2,645.2 hours of sunshine per year. The largest number of sunny days are in July (368.1 hours) and the smallest number in December and January (110.3 and 113.6 hours respectively).

The main crops in the Greater District of Thessaloniki are: cotton (50-25%), grains (44-38%), vegetables (16-15%), oats, barley, rice and grapes.

In terms of financial strength and production volume, Thessaloniki is the second – after Athens – largest city in Greece. Thessaloniki's role in the production sector is primary as demonstrated by: the extent of commercial transactions, the amount of industrial production and the exports to other countries. Jobs in this field amount to 44.3% as opposed to 40.5% in Athens, and 43.1% in Patras. The

A sculpture on the waterfront in Thessaloniki

as well as its prominent geopolitical position, make Thessaloniki a centre of attraction in the Balkans, Central Europe, the Near East and Africa. Moreover, Thessaloniki constitutes a nucleus of industrial development in Northern Greece, presenting a streamlined administrative, political, and cultural organization.

A projection based on present conditions (with a corresponding overall development and the required support by the state) envisages a city in the year 2000 with a population of 1.100.000.

increase in the industrial workforce reached 42.3% within a four-year period (1969-1973). The main industrial areas of Thessaloniki are: Diavata, Sindos, Kalohori, Langada, Oreokastro, as well as the University School of Agriculture, and Thermi.

The modern industrial units, the land-sea-and-air transport network, the immense potential of its port, the fertile Macedonian mainland, the International Fair (HELEXPO) (with its specialized exhibitions throughout the year),

→
The OTE (Telecommunications) tower

A view of the old waterfront

Thessaloniki: History

Thessaloniki which celebrated its 2300th anniversary in 1985 has a long, rich, and uninterrupted history. In 315 B.C., it was founded by the king of Macedonia, Cassander, and for the next 23 centuries it has always played a leading role in the Balkans as the bulwark of Hellenism.

Thessaloniki, the "metropolis" of Macedonia throughout the centuries, which Cassander built in the bay of Thermaikos, holds a prominent geopolitical position.

This new city, named after the

Statue of Alexander the Great on the waterfront in Thessaloniki

→
A view of the waterfront

sister of Alexander the Great, was created by the incorporation of 26 communities (polismata) in the bay of Thermaikos. Herodotus (5th century BC) in his description of Xerxes' campaign against Greece ("Polymnia") mentions Therme as the main city in the area. Archaeological excavations in the centre of the city have brought to light the imposing ruins of an ancient Ionian temple which prove the uniformity of Ionian culture throughout the ancient Greek mainland and islands.

The historian and geographer, Strabo (1st century BC), in his "Geographica", provides

information on Thessaloniki describing it as the "metropolis of Macedonia".

Excavations carried out in Thessaloniki and its greater area prove that this area was first inhabited some 5,000 year ago. Finds, bearing strong neolithic characteristics, were discovered in the "toumba" (prehistoric tumulus) in east Thessaloniki and date to the early and middle Bronze Age (3000 - 1600 BC). According to Herodotus, these prehistoric settlements did not only survive the Iron Age (1000 BC), but were in existence as cities during the 5th century BC (Aenea, Sindos, and Chalastra). Settlement of the area of the gulf of Thermaikos reached its peak during the Macedonian dynasty. Ancient tradition has it, that these were descendants of Dorian Temenos, who founded the royal Argead dynasty or Temenides in ancient Macedonia.

The Macedonians were a Dorian Greek race, which originally settled in the mountains

The waterfront in Thessaloniki (beginning of the century postcard)

SALONICCO - Lo scalo
SALONIQUE - Le quai
SALONICA - The Quay

of Macedonia, and later gradually moved to the coast of Pieria and the gulf of Thermaikos, especially during the reign of Amyntas I, king of Macedonia (520-500 BC).

With the ascendancy to the throne of Philip II (359-336 BC), the Macedonians took control of mainland Greece and established a unified Greek "state of cities" in contrast to the existing Greek "city-states". Philip's policy was carried on by his son, Alexander the Great, when he succeeded him to the throne.

In 334 B.C., Alexander the Great, king of Macedonia, and an undisputed leader of all Greeks, undertook his great campaign against the Persians and their allies who posed a continuous threat in the East. Alexander left behind the elderly general, Antipater (397-319 BC), as regent-in-charge. Antipater's authority extended not only over Macedonia, but southern Greece as well, on the principle of the "koinou ton Ellinon". Alexander's death on 10 June 323 B.C. in

The White Tower soon after the liberation of the city

Bronze coins of Cassander's reign (4th century)

The city of Thessaloniki as represented on a marble apse of the Galerius palace group of buildings

Babylon was followed by "the wars of the successors" to his vast empire. After a long struggle, Cassander, the eldest son of Antipater, prevailed in Macedonia in 316 B.C. In 315 B.C., Cassander founded the city of Thessaloniki, naming it after his wife who was the sister of Alexander the Great.

Thessaloniki quickly developed into a safe, fortified city. This fact was appreciated by Antigonus, king of Macedonia, who, 30 years after its founding, made Thessaloniki his base in his defence against the king of Epirus, Pyrrhos. The city's importance during the Hellenistic period becomes evident, when considering that, in 279 B.C., even the Celts attacked it in force. They were successfully repulsed before the city walls in a battle during which the king of Macedonia, Ptolemy Keraunos (281-279 BC), was killed. Since that time, Thessaloniki, the main port in Macedonia, became one of the most important military bases, due to its commanding position. In 169 B.C., Thessaloniki was

$\rightarrow$
The White Tower

Perseus, the last of the Macedonian kings

Statue of the Roman emperor Augustus (27 B.C. - A.D. 14) - Archaeological Museum of Thessaloniki

unsuccessfully besieged by the Romans. A year later, though, it followed the fate of the other Greek cities, when Perseus, king of Macedonia, was defeated by the legions of Aemilius Paulus at Pydna.

During the period of Roman rule, Thessaloniki prospered within the sphere of "Pax Romana". Macedonia was then devided into four regions (regiones) and Thessaloniki became the capital of the second region (Macedonia Secunda). After 148 B.C., these four regions were consolidated into "Provincia Macedonia". Thessaloniki was the capital of this new province, which expanded to include the whole of southern Greece, and it retained its boundaries up until the rule of Augustus (27 B.C.).

Thessaloniki, now considered "the mother of all Macedonia", went through a period of commercial, industrial, and cultural development and held a commanding position over the whole of the Haemus peninsula. The city retained its Greek character, a fact which is documented by the numerous finds of the period (inscriptions, coins, etc) and the account given by the Roman orator, Cicero, who visited the city in 58 B.C. During the Roman civil war which followed (49-31 B.C.), Macedonia became the centre of conflict between the Republicans and the supporters of Caesar. Thessaloniki, took the side of Antonius and Octavian and honoured the victors of the battle of Philippi (42 B.C.) by erecting an imposing triumphal arch at the gate of Axios. As a reward, Thessaloniki was granted the status of a "free city" (Liberam Civitatem) and was given many privileges and what amounted to

Part of the city of Thessaloniki

self-government. The Olympian and Pythian Games were celebrated with equal splendour to the games of ancient Olympia, while famous artists, writers, poets and orators taught in the city.

The city continued to flourish during the 1st century A.D. , which might be the reason why Saint Paul chose it to preach the new faith and establish a Christian church (A.D. 50). It is to the people of the city of Thessaloniki, which Paul calls the "Golden Gate to Europe" for Christianity, that he addressed his well-known epistles which constitute two of the most important texts in the Christian faith.

Thessaloniki was at its prime during the rule of Caesar Galerius, brother-in-law of Diocletian and a member of the Roman tetrarchate. Galerius was appointed governor of Illyricum (Balkans) and chose Thessaloniki as his base (beginning of the 4th

The main gate at the Vardari fortress (Top Hane)

century). The most imposing Roman buildings were erected during this period, such as: the Rotunda, Galerius' Arch of Triumph (Kamara), the Palace, the Ancient Agora (Forum), etc. The main thoroughfare, which ran through the city and parallel to the waterfront, was Via Egnatia which started from the "Golden Gate" (Axios Gate/Chrisi Pyli - present-day Demokratias square) and ended at the Cassandreotiki Gate (Kalamaria Gate - present-day Syntrivani square). Another road parallel to Via Egnatia (present-day Aghiou Demetriou street) started from the "Litaea Gate" of the west walls and ended at the "New Golden Gate" (Nea Chrysi Pyli) in the east. It is possible that yet another road vertical to the above (present-day Venizelou street) led from the port to the Acropolis in the Upper City (Ano Poli). There is archaeological evidence that there were Roman cemeteries outside the walls, to

The walls along Acropolis street

→

Aristotelous square

the east and west of the city, in approximately the same location as those of the Hellenistic period.

In the beginning of the 4th century, the "protector" and patron saint of Thessaloniki, Demetrius, and his friend Nestor, met a martyr's death. Since then, Thessaloniki has become the centre of worship of Saint Demetrius throughout the Christian world. The decline of the Roman Empire began after Diocletian and Maximian retired from power and Constantine the Great chose Thessaloniki as his base in the preparations for his confrontation with his brother-in-law, Licinius (313). As Zosimos relates, in 324, Constantine brought his great army of 120,000 men into the city and built a new port (in place of the old Roman port) to facilitate his armada of 200 galleys and 2000 merchant ships. Once Constantine won the war and established himself as the sole ruler of the Roman

Statue of Alexander the Great

Empire, where Christianity became the officially accepted faith, he made Byzantium (the old colony of Megara in Propontis) the new capital of the Roman state under the name of Constantinople or New Rome. Constantinople and Thessaloniki became the dominant cities in the Byzantine empire for the next 1000 years. Constantinople was, thus, the reigning city (vasilevousa) and Thessaloniki the co-reigning city or joint capital (symvasilevousa) of the mighty Eastern state ("Thessaloniki, second to the greatest Roman city", "the eye of Europe and of Greece in particular"). An important period for the city was during the rule of Julian the Apostate (361-363) and Theodosius the Great (379-395) when it became the base for their wars against the Goths. In 390, 7,000 citizens of the city were slaughtered in the Hippodrome on emperor Theodosius' orders when they rioted against Theodosius' Goth garrison and its commander, Vuterichus.

During the following centuries (395-695), Thessaloniki faced the frequent Goth raids of Alaric and Theodoric, of Slavs who advanced south from the Carpathians, of the mongolian Avars, of the Draguvites, Sagudates, Velegezites, Vaiunites, and Verzites. The emperor Justinian II the Rhinotmetus put an end to the continuous threats of invasion by decisively defeating the Slavs and entering Thessaloniki in triumph - an event which has been preserved in a wall-painting of the church of St. Demetrius. A long period of peace follows as Byzantium gradually establishes a Greek national identity. It is from Thessaloniki, this influential centre of culture, that Cyril and

The White Tower

Methodius, the two Thessalonian theologians, set out on their mission to Bulgaria, Syria, Moravia, and the land of the Khazars. During the rule of Michael III (842-867), they helped spread Christianity among these people and greatly contributed towards their cultural development.

In 904, after a long period of peace, Thessaloniki is caught unprepared by the onslaught of Saracen Arabs. These pirates captured the city and mercilessly plundered it for days despite the valiant resistance of its citizens. Nevertheless, the city survived and quickly recovered to face 100 years of Bulgar attacks. In 1014, these attacks came to an end, when the emperor Basil II (976-1025) decisively defeated the Bulgars at Strymon. Thus, began a new period of prosperity for Thessaloniki and the whole of Macedonia. During this time, the "Demetria" celebrations, a religious and folk festival in honour of St. Demetrius, the city's patron saint, were established. These were held in the city, as well as west of the city on the plain of Axios, every October. A large trade fair which attracted tradesmen from the whole of the empire, as well as Italy, Egypt, Spain, Phoenicia, the Black Sea, etc., was also part of the "Demetria" festival.

The death of Basil II heralded the beginning of the decline and collapse of Byzantium. The Normans now lay siege to Thessaloniki (1185) with an army of 80,000 men and 200 ships. The virtually undefended city was captured and once again plundered. The whole of the Byzantine empire soon broke up in the hands of the Latin crusaders of the West and, in 1204, Thessaloniki found itself the capital of a Latin kingdom under the Italian, Boniface of Montferrat. For the next twenty years, Thessaloniki greatly suffered under the crusaders, who had forgotten their ultimate goal, the "freeing" of the Holy Land.

In Thessaloniki, Latin rule came to an end when Theodore Angelus Comnenus, the "despot" of Epirus, proclaimed himself "king and emperor of the Romans" and created the Greek empire of Thessaloniki (1224-1246). In 1261, Michael Palaeologus ended the Latin occupation of Constantinople. Byzantium, though, defensively weakened and territorially restricted, could not stop the advance of the Ottoman Turks, who soon reached Europe.

The next threat that Thessaloniki now faced came from the Serbs and the Catalans. The Catalans, mercenaries in the army, after plundering Thrace, East Macedonia, and Mt. Athos, besieged Thessaloniki, in 1308, fortunately without success.

Relief representations, Kamara (Galerius Arch), Thessaloniki

During the 14th century, Constantinople was unable to offer any help and Thessaloniki had to fend for itself in these difficult circumstances. Although militarily weak, the city not only survived but went through a "golden age" during the first half of the 14th century. Thessaloniki, which the metropolitan (archbishop) Nicolaos Kavasilas called "a city common to the whole of Greece", became the centre of culture of Hellenism, and its people enjoyed full self-rule, independence, and social justice. Philosophers, legislators, and theologians, such as Constantine Armenopoulos, Matthew Blastares, Gregory Palamas, Thomas Magister, Nicolaos Kavasilas, Nicephoros Humnos, Demetrios and Prochoros Cydones, etc., created a renaissance in culture during the Palaeologi era in Thessaloniki. Architecture and church building equally flourished as surviving monuments of the period show, such as, Aghia Ekaterini, Aghioi

Kamara (Galerius Arch) in Thessaloniki

The church of Aghioi Apostoloi (Holy Apostles)

Apostoloi, Aghios Nicolaos Orphanos, Prophitis Elias, Aghios Panteleimon, Taxiarches, Metamorphosi Sotira, and the Monastery of Vlatadon. Manuel Panselinos, the famous icon-painter, lived and worked in Thessaloniki at the end of the 13th and beginning of the 14th century. Many icon-painters "graduated" from the well-known workshops in Thessaloniki and Mt. Athos.

Two important events took place during the 14th century in Thessaloniki: the well-known "Hesychasm" controversy between Gregory Palamas (orator, philosopher, theologian, and later metropolitan of Thessaloniki) and Barlaam (the enlightened Greek monk from Calabria in southern Italy); and the "Zealots" movement/uprising (1342-1349), which made Thessaloniki into an independent commune ("people's republic") at a time of feudal prosperity.

Civil war in Byzantium (1321-1328) allowed parts of the empire

Hosios David (The Monastery of Latomou)

to fall into the hands of foreign invaders and, despite the desperate measures taken by Manuel Palaeologus, the then "despot" of Thessaloniki and later emperor of Byzantium, this signalled the beginning of the end for the empire. When Andronicus, the "despot" of Thessaloniki, fell ill, the city decided to surrender to the Venetians under certain conditions, in order to avoid being occupied by the Turks of Murad II (1421-1451). These conditions stated that the people of the city would enjoy complete freedom and Thessaloniki would be reinforced to withstand any Turkish attacks. Unfortunately, the Venetians did not adhere to the agreement and the city fell to the Turks, after a ruthless siege, on 28 March 1430. The capture of Thessaloniki was followed by that of Constantinople on 29 May 1453. The fall of the two bastions of Hellenism and Christianity opened the way for the Turks to the rest of the Balkan peninsula and central Europe.

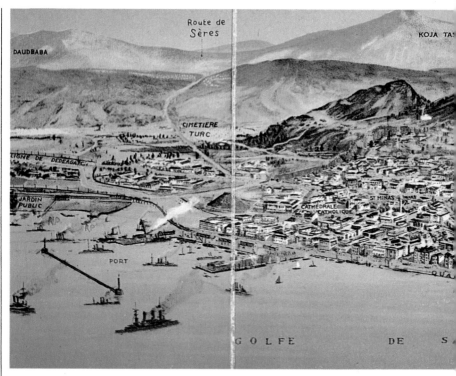

Panoramic view of Thessaloniki

The Turks plundered and almost destroyed the whole city. Thousands of its inhabitants were caught prisoner and were led chain-bound to the slave markets of the East, leaving the city deserted. The main Byzantine churches were taken over and converted into mosques. The houses of the wealthy were requisitioned by Turkish officers and the rest were given to Turkish irregulars and other "adventurers" attracted to the city by the spoils of war. Special measures had to be taken by the Turks to encourage the return of the inhabitants of the city in the hope of a better future. The city gradually recovered and once again became one of the busy ports in the Balkans. Furthermore, during the 15th century, a great number of Jewish refugees from the West came to Thessaloniki. They formed an active community which greatly contributed to the development of commerce and

On the image: (ANCIEN FOR, ANCIENNE VILLE, Eglise de St Elias, KONAK, Eglise de S. Dimitris, Eglise S. George, Eglise Saint Sophie, Arc de Triomphe de Galerius, Eglise Metropolitaine, BOULEVARD HAMIDIE, QUARTIER, I Q U E

→
Thessaloniki at night

shipping.

The "awakening" of the subjugated peoples of Europe and the beginning of the disintegration of Ottoman rule followed the defeat of Sultan Mehmed IV at the siege of Vienna by the Poles and the Germans in 1683. Thessaloniki revolted against the Turks at least five times up to 1789.

Thessaloniki and the whole of Macedonia played a decisive part in the Greek Revolution of 1821.

When Emmanuel Papas triggered off the uprising in neighbouring Chalkidiki, the Turks turned their fury against the defenceless population of Thessaloniki (17 May 1821). At least 3,000 people together with the city notables were slaughtered at the "Konak" (Government House), the dungeon of Kanli Kule, and the enclosure of Gregory Palamas church. When massacre and persecution came to an end and the newly-founded Greek State

An icon-painting workshop in Thessaloniki

determination for the liberation and independence of Macedonia which had always had a homogenous Greek population.

Thessaloniki was liberated by the Greek army soon after the beginning of the First Balkan war on the day of St. Demetrius, patron saint of the city (26 October 1912).

was established in the south, peace returned to Thessaloniki and the city regained its prosperity.

In 1869, during the reorganization of the empire, which was imposed on the Turks by the European powers, the east and sea-front Byzantine walls were demolished and the fear-inspiring Kanli-Kule tower (Tower of Blood) was white-washed and renamed White Tower. Furthermore, many new streets were built as well as government and public buildings. The struggle for independence of the Greek regions in the north continued well into the beginning of the 20th century. The Macedonian Struggle (1904-1908) demonstrated Greek

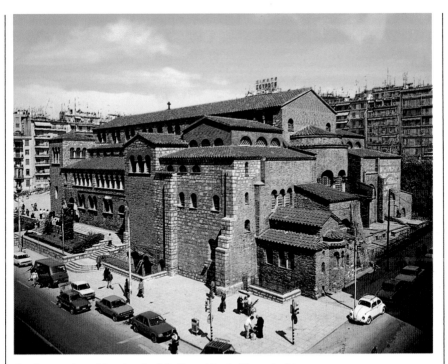

South-east view of the church of St. Demetrius in Thessaloniki

→
*St. Demetrius on a wall-painting in the
church of Aghios Nicolaos Orphanos in
Thessaloniki*

The Acropolis Byzantine walls. The tower of Trigoniou in the background

Thessaloniki: Monuments

The walls of Thessaloniki were built just after its founding by Cassander in 315 B.C. The walls form a rectangle with its east and south sides perpendicular to the sea-front. The sea-front walls were demolished during the last period of Turkish occupation. In the upper section of the walls is the Acropolis and the Heptapyrgio fortress. The main fortification work of the city was carried out by emperor Theodosius the Great (379-395) while construction work continued during the reign of the emperors Zeno (474-491), Anastasius I (491-518), and Leo the Wise (886-912). Minor additions were made by Basil II Boulgaroctonus (976-1025) as well as in the 14th century during the Palaeologi era.

The best known gates in the city walls were "The Gate of Rome" (near the White Tower), "The Kassandreotiki Gate" (part of it survives at present-day Syntrivani square), "The Litea Gate", "The Pseudochrysi Gate" (at the east and west end of

View from the Heptapyrgion walls

present-day Aghiou Demetriou street), "The Axios Gate" or "Chrysi Gate" (Golden Gate, at present-day Demokratias square), "The Yalu Gate" (near the seafront), and the "The Anna Palaeologina Gate" (which survives intact next to the Tower of Trigoniou at the Acropolis in the Upper City). The well-known White Tower was part of the city walls and was erected on the site

The tower of Manuel. Byzantine walls of Thessaloniki

Ancient Agora (Forum). Part of the cryptoporticus in the south of the square (foreground).

of an old Byzantine tower during the end of Venetian rule or perhaps a little later.

The Ancient Agora (Forum)

The Forum was most probably built on the site of the Ancient Agora of the Hellenistic period which was a social and religious centre with imposing and magnificent public buildings. It is argued that buildings of the Roman period in the Ancient Agora (Forum) were erected during 42 B.C - A.D. 138, while the main buildings are of the Roman Tetrarchate (end of the 3rd - beginning of the 4th century).

What has survived in the Agora are: part of the flagstone paved square, a conservatoire with brick stands, the ground floor of a cryptoporticus (multi-storey gallery), mosaic floors, cobble streets, etc.

The Rotunda

The Rotunda, located to the north of Egnatia street, is part of the Galerius Arch of Triumph (Kamara) and the Roman Palace

Rotunda (Aghios Georgios) in Thessaloniki

(at present-day Navarinou square) forming a unified group of monuments. The Rotunda is a circular building with 6.3 m thick walls and a brick dome 24.5 m in diameter. The prevailing view is that it was either built as an imperial mausoleum or a temple dedicated to the god Cabeirus. During the reign of Theodosius the Great (379-395), the sanctuary at the east niche was added, together with the 8 m wide circular transept, the foundations of which still survive.

The interior was of coloured marble revetment and mosaics. The exquisite mosaics of the dome can still be seen, as well as parts of those in the arches of the niches.

Egnatia street. Galerius Arch (Kamara) on the right.

$\longrightarrow$
The east Byzantine walls of Thessaloniki

The Galerius Arch of Triumph (Kamara)

The Galerius Arch of Triumph is situated to the east of Egnatia street between the Rotunda and the Roman palace and constituted the west part of a covered market which joined these two buildings. It was built in the beginning of the 4th century in honour of emperor Galerius upon his triumphal return from his victorious campaign against the Persians. It is decorated with marble reliefs, decorative anthemia, and festoons of leaves. (At the west end of Egnatia street there stood another triumphal arch to honour the victors of the battle of Philippi (A.D. 42), Antonius and Octavian).

The Roman Palace at Navarinou square

The Roman Palace - The Hippodrome

Part of the imposing Roman Palace survives south of the Arch of Galerius (present-day Navarinou square) which was built around an open court.

In the Palace, a number of important mosaic floors were unearthed as well as a marble apse with relief portraits of Galerius and Thessaloniki (Archaeological Museum of Thessaloniki).

An octagonal chamber with seven recesses in its interior is connected to the south-west side of the Palace. The use of the "Octagon" has not been established, but could have served as Galerius' throne chamber.

Part of the ancient Roman Hippodrome (Circus) was discovered east of the Roman Palace and along one side of present-day Hippodromiou square together with ruins of arches of the west side which were most probably part of vaulted passages (carceres).

This was the place where, in 390, when the citizens of the city revolted against the Goth

View of the city from the Sailing Club

garrison, some 7,000 Thessalonians were slaughtered on the orders of Theodosius the Great.

Both the Palace and the Hippodrome were built during the time of the Tetrarchate (297-307).

St. Demetrius

St. Demetrius church is located north-east of the Ancient Agora, on present-day Aghiou Demetriou street, and is the monument particularly associated with the fortunes of the city, as it is dedicated to its patron saint, St. Demetrius.

The original church was built (c. 413) by Leontius, prefect of Illyricum, on the site of a chapel dedicated to the "myrovlites" St. Demetrius. It is of the five-aisled basilica style, the so-called Hellenistic. On the west side of its court there was an open "peristyle" (atrium) with a marble covered fountain (phiale) at its centre. During the years 629-634, the church was restored by emperor Heraclius after having been destroyed in a fire.

In the 13th century, during the rule of emperor Michael VIII Palaeologus, the church was

The catacombs in the church of St. Demetrius in Thessaloniki

→
The church of St. Demetrius in Thessaloniki

radically repaired and the small chapel of St. Efthymios was built. The wall-paintings in the chapel are attributed to Panselinos. The church of St. Demetrius contains important mosaics depicting the life of the saint.

The church was almost completely destroyed during the great fire of 1917 and restored in 1949. The remains of St.

St. Demetrius and two children. A 7th century mosaic in the church of St. Demetrius

The ancient tradition of the copersmiths still survives

Demetrius are preserved in a special reliquary in the church.

Acheiropoietos

The church of Acheiropoietos is in the centre of the city, north of Egnatia street, and opposite Makedonomachon square.

It is a wooden roofed, three-aisled basilica of the "hellenistic" style and, together with the churches of St. Demetrius and Aghia Sophia, it constitutes an example of early Christian church architecture. It is believed that the church was built directly after the Third Ecumenical Council at Ephesus (431). It is dedicated to the Virgin Mary and it took its name from the "acheiropoietos" (not made by human hands) icon of the "Theotokos" (Virgin Mary).

The church contains important early Christian mosaics on the soffits of the colonnade as well as an inscription by the conqueror of Thessaloniki, Murad II, carved on a marble column of the north aisle.

Hosios David (Monastery of Latomou)

The church of Hosios David is located in the Upper City (Ano Poli), south-west of the Monastery of Vlatadon.

It was probably built in the end of the 5th or beginning of the 6th century, and was the "forerunner" of the "cross-shaped" church with a dome which appeared much later.

This small church, which underwent a number of alterations during the Turkish occupation, was the "katholikon"* of a monastery during the early part of the 9th century.

Of great interest is the well-known mosaic in the apse of the sanctuary and its 12th century wall-paintings.

---

*The "katholikon" is the central part of the church, i.e. the area between the sanctuary and the narthex and, therefore, constitutes the main church of a monastery.

West view of the church of Aghia Sophia in Thessaloniki

Aghia Sophia

The church of Aghia Sophia is in the centre of the city, south of Egnatia street, and a small distance from the church of Acheiropoietos.

The building is considered to be a "domed basilica" in the transitional style prior to that of a "cruciform domed basilica". It was dedicated to Christ (as was Haghia Sophia in Constantinople with which it shares many characteristics) and was built after the First Ecumenical Council of Nicaea (325) when Christ was acknowledged as the "Word and Wisdom of God".

According to prevailing views, the mosaics in the dome and the apse of the sanctuary are of the same age as the church.

During the Turkish rule, alterations to the church changed its exterior.

Panagia Halkeon

The church of Panagia Halkeon is located north of Egnatia street, near the Ancient Agora, in the area of the "halkadika" (coppersmith shops)

The church of Panagia Halkeon

→
The church of Aghia Ekaterini

which date back to Byzantine times.

It is of the cruciform style with a dome and is distinguished for the elegance of its brick walls. According to an inscription carved on the marble lintel over the west

←
The interior of the church of Aghia Sophia in Thessaloniki

entrance, the church was built by the "protospatharios" Christophoros on a site where once stood an ancient temple dedicated to Hephaestus or Cabeirus.

In the church there are important wall-paintings as well as the grave of its founder, Christophoros.

Part of the west side of the church of Aghia Ekaterini

Aghia Ekaterini

The church of Aghia Ekaterini in the north-west part of the Upper City (Ano Poli), near the Byzantine walls, belongs to the so-called "Macedonian School" style. It was built in the end of the 13th century and its architecture and wall-paintings are of great interest.

Aghioi Apostoloi (Holy Apostles)

The church of Aghioi Apostoloi is located south of the church of Aghia Ekaterini and almost adjacent to the west walls.

It is a cruciform church with a dome, like Aghia Ekaterini, ("Macedonian School") and was the "katholikon" of a monastery founded by Patriarch Nephon I (1312-1315).

Its walls, mosaics, and wall-paintings are unique examples of the Palaeologi period (14th century).

Aghios Nicolaos Orphanos

The small church of Aghios Nicolaos Orphanos is situated at the end of Apostolou Pavlou street, south of Kalithea square in the Upper City (Ano Poli).

It is a single-aisled basilica with a gallery and was the "katholikon" of a monastery (a "metochi" of the monastery of Vlatadon). Part of its vestibule survives on present-day Herodotou street. The wall construction of this small church places it in the first half of the 14th century. The whole of its interior is decorated with exquisite wall-paintings.

Aghios Panteleimon

The church of Aghios Panteleimon is located north of Egnatia street, near the Arch of Galerius, on the site of the Byzantine monastery of Perivleptos or "kyr-Isaak" and served as its "katholikon".

It was one of the first churches to be built in the "Macedonian School" style during the Palaeologi era. It is an interesting building with few, but important, wall-paintings.

↑ *The church of Aghios Nicolaos Orphanos*   *The church of Metamorphosis Sotira* ↓

The "katholikon" of the Monastery of Vlatadon

Prophitis Elias

The church of Prophitis Elias is located in the north-west of the Upper City (Ano Poli), between Aghiou Demetriou street and Athinas street (Olympiados), behind the "Diikitirio".

It is a cruciform church with a dome and a large square narthex called "liti". Like the churches on Mt. Athos, it was built c. 1360 by Macarios Houmnos as the "katholikon" of the Nea Moni (New Monastery). There is evidence that this church was built on the site of the Byzantine palace (vasileia) which was destroyed during the Zealots uprising (1342-1349).

Besides its interesting architecture, the church also contains wall-paintings in the narthex.

The Monastery of Vlatadon

The Monastery of Vlatadon is at the top of the Upper City (Ano Poli), on Heptapyrgiou street, near the Acropolis.

Tradition has it, that the church was built by the monks Dorotheos and Markos Vlatis as the "katholikon" of the Monastery of Vlatadon sometime between 1351-1371 with the support of the empress, Anna Palaeologina. Despite the various alterations to the original building, it remains a "cruciform" style church, like the churches of Aghia Ekaterini and Aghioi Apostoloi. The church, which is dedicated to the "Pantocrator" (Almighty), contains important wall-paintings. Also of interest are the Abbey (more recent) and the chapel of the Assumption of the Virgin Mary (Koimisis tis Theotokou).

Taxiarhes

The church of Taxiarhes is situated in the north-east part of the Upper City (Ano Poli), south of Acropoleos street.

The church of Nea Panagia

Although greatly altered through later additions, the church must have originally been a basilica with a gallery on its three sides. It may have served as the "katholikon" of a monastery built sometime in the 14th century.

East view of the church of Taxiarhes

Metamorphosi Sotira (Transfiguration of the Saviour)

The church of Metamorphosi Sotira is located south-west of Galerius Arch and south of Egnatia street.

This small and elegant church most probably constituted part of the monastery "of Joel" (kyr-Ioil)

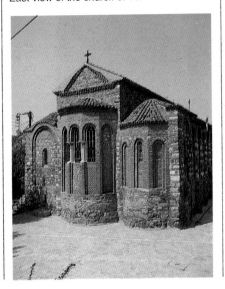

The south-west side of the church of Prophitis Elias

View of the city from the Monastery of Vlatadon

and must have been built during the first half of the 14th century in the Palaeologi era.

Churches of more recent origin

Also noteworthy are the churches built during the period of Turkish occupation. These include:

Aghios Minas (on I. Dragoumi street) built after the fire of 1839 on the site of a 15th century church.

Panagia Lagoudiani or Laodigitria (between Kassandrou street and Athinas street) built on the site of the Byzantine monastery of Panagia.

Ypapanti (adjacent to the church of Metamorphosi Sotira) built on the site of the monastery "of Joel".

Aghios Georgios (west of the Rotunda) was a one-time "metochi" of the Monastery of Gregoriou on Mt. Athos.

Panagouda (west of the Rotunda) was closely associated with the Greek community of the city during the Turkish rule.

Aghios Athanasios (near the church of Acheiropoietos on Egnatia street) was built in 1818.

Nea Panagia (south of Tsimiski street, near the White Tower) was possibly built on the site of the 14th century monastery of Theotokos.

Aghios Antonios (at the intersection of D. Margariti street

South side of the Bey-Hamami in Thessaloniki

and Philikis Eterias street) was built during the second half of the 19th century.

Muslim Monuments

A number of notable Muslim monuments constructed during the Turkish occupation (1430-1912) are still to be found in Thessaloniki. Among them are:

Hamza Bey Cami (at the intersection of Egnatia st. and Venizelou st.) built c. 1468.

Alaca Imaret Cami (in a small road off Kassandrou street) built by Ishak Pasa in 1500.

Yeni Cami (on Archaeologikou Mouseiou st., in east Thessaloniki) built in 1902 by the Italian architect, Vitaliano Poselli

Yahudi Hamami (between Kominon st. and Vas. Irakliou st.) possibly built during the first half of the 16th century.

Bey Hamami (corner of Egnatia st. and Metropolitou Gennadiou st.) built in 1444 by the Sultan Murad II.

Pasa Hamami (on Peniou, Kalvou, and P. Karatza streets) built sometime between 1520 and 1566 by the Turkish governor of Thessaloniki, Cezeri.

Bezesten (Fabric Marketplace

↑ *Hamza-bey Cami in Thessaloniki*

Bezesten in Thessaloniki ↓

Yahudi Hamami in Thessaloniki

Alaca Imaret in Thessaloniki

Yeni Cami (the old Archaeological Museum) in Thessaloniki

on Venizelou st) built by Bayezid II during the end of the 15th century.

Yeni Hamami (intersection of Kassandrou and Ag. Demetriou st.) possibly built in the last quarter of the 16th century.

Popular Architecture - Neoclassical Buildings

In addition to the Hellenistic, Roman, and Byzantine monuments in Thessaloniki, there are buildings of the traditional "popular Macedonian" as well as the modern period "neoclassical" architecture.

The great fire of 1917 destroyed the old city centre in addition to numerous buildings of traditional architecture. Nevertheless, many important buildings survived in the Upper City (Ano Poli), and have now been listed, which bear the features of traditional architecture, such as sheltered balconies and projecting windows ("hayatia" and "sahnisia"). A visit to the Upper City (Ano Poli) offers cobble-stone streets, cul-de-sacs, pleasant small clearings, and an excellent view of Thessaloniki. Some of the more picturesque streets are:

View of the Upper City

Demetriou Poliorkiti, Alexandrou Papadopoulou, Theophilou, Antiohou, Amphitriona, Herodotou, Sahtouri, Acropoleos.

Neoclassical buildings of the modern period are situated in the centre and east part of the city. They are known as "pyrgoi" (castles) and originally belonged to wealthy citizens of the city. Some of these buildings are:

The old Greek Consulate (Aghia Sophias & Proxenou

Buildings in the popular Macedonian architecture in the Upper City

Athinas, Olympiados, and Herodotou streets in the Upper City (painting by M. Zafeiriadis)

Koromila streets) which now houses the Museum of the Macedonian Struggle.

Diikitirio (Government House at Aghiou Demetriou-Venizelou st.)

The School of Philosophy building at the University of Thessaloniki (Ethnikis Amynis st).

The old Municipal Hospital (Kastron st.)

The 3rd Army Corps HQ building (Leoforos Stratou st.)

The Papafio Orphanage

Cobblestone street in the Upper City

The Villa Allatini (present-day Prefecture of Thessaloniki)

building (Papafi st.)
    The Customs House (docks)
    The Municipal Gallery (Leof.
Vas. Olgas - 25 March st.)
    The Prefecture building (Leof.
Vas. Olgas - Ploutonos st.)

$\longrightarrow$
The old E΄ High School of Thessaloniki (Villa Ahmed Kapatzi) after its restoration. It is currently used as a cultural centre.

Reliefs on a larnax (Archaeological Museum of Thessaloniki)

Museums - Galleries - Art Collections

Archaeological Museum (Y.M.C.A. square)

The museum exhibits include: fossils and pots of the prehistoric period, sculptures of the Hellenistic and pre-Roman times, inscriptions, sarcophagi, Roman sculptures, small copper and clay idols, remains of buildings, and mosaics.

The findings on exhibit from the Royal Tombs in Vergina are unique. The gold larnax, the gold wreath, the ivory-gold shield of king Philip II, a piece of fabric, the Macedonian iron helmet, etc.

Also of interest are the findings of Sindos (5th and 4th century BC) as well as those of Derveni where the excellent bronze krater (c.330 BC) was found.

The Museum of Byzantine Culture

A newly-founded museum to serve the preservation, research, study, and promotion of Byzantine culture in Macedonia and Thessaloniki, in particular, - a city

The Papafeio Orphanage in Thessaloniki

The White Tower Museum

The museum operates under the authority of the Directorate of Byzantine antiquities and contains exhibits covering the period A.D. 400 - 1430. The most important of these are: a reconstruction of the fortifications and walls of Thessaloniki during the Byzantine period, models of the main styles of churches including decorative elements (capitals, mosaics, votive vessels), funerary offerings, pieces of sculpture, tombstones, pots, jewellery, maps, and icons.

Folk Life and Ethnological Museum of Macedonia (Leof. Vas. Olgas - Philippou Nicoglou st.)

The museum is housed in an excellent 1906 neoclassical building and contains some 8,000 items including objects of daily use, household furniture and utensils, models of houses in the traditional "Popular Macedonian" architectural style, costumes, jewellery, gold embroidery, vestments, ceramics, silvercraft and metallcraft objects. (Of particular interest is a reconstruction of a typical middle-class home in Thessaloniki in the beginning of the century).

which was only second to Constantinople during the Byzantine Empire.

The museum provides space for permanent exhibitions of items relating to various aspects of life during the Byzantine period, such as: family, religion, society, culture, art, etc. Special exhibitions with subject-related events are also frequently held on the premises. Moreover, the museum plans to house collections of Byzantine and post-Byzantine icons, coins, ceramics, miniature art, etc.

Folk Life and Ethnological Museum of Macedonia (Megalou Alexandrou Avenue)

The Municipal Gallery (at the intersection of Vas. Olgas and Martiou streets)

Museum of the Macedonian Struggle (Aghias Sofias - Prox. Koromila st.)

The museum is housed in a 19th century neoclassical building which was the Greek Consulate during the Turkish occupation and the base for the "Macedonian Struggle" for the liberation of Macedonia (1904-1908).

On exhibit are documents relating to the "Macedonian Struggle", items belonging to Pavlos Melas and the metropolitan (archbishop) Germanos Karavangelis, uniforms and guns of the "Makedonomachoi" (Macedonian fighters), portraits, photographs, and plans of battle.

Municipal Gallery (Leof. Vas. Olgas - 25 Martiou st.)

The gallery is housed in a 1905 neoclassical building, property of the Municipality of Thessaloniki. The exhibits include paintings and sculptures by modern artists, mainly from Thessaloniki (P. Rengos, N. Fotakis, Ch. Lefakis, N.G. Pentzikis, N. Sahinis, I. Svoronos, F. Zoglopitis, L. Venetoulias, S. Mavrommatis, K. Tsizek, N. Kesanlis, K. Loustas, K. Demetriadi-Natsi, P. Papanakos, G. Kontaxakis, L. Christidou, P. Paralis, S. Servopoulos, K. Kambadakis, etc).

→
A mansion in the district of "Exohes" (105 Vas. Olgas st.). It now houses the Organization for the Cultural Capital of Europe "Thessaloniki '97".

The waterfront

The Telogleio Foundation Gallery

The gallery owns a collection of some 3,000 paintings, sculptures, gold and silver articles. The collection will be housed in the "Telogleio Foundation" building which is still under construction, on the University campus.

The University of Thessaloniki Portrait Collection

This collection is housed in the School of Philosophy building of the University of Thessaloniki and contains portraits of university rectors and professors painted by well-known Greek artists.

The Institute of Macedonian Studies Theatre

Thessaloniki: Events

"Demetria"

A wide-range of cultural events organized in October every year by the Municipality of Thessaloniki, carrying on the tradition of the 12th century Byzantine "Demetria".

"Greek Song Festival"

An annual contest of Greek modern songs organized by the International Fair of Thessaloniki in the middle of September.

"The Film Festival of Thessaloniki"

An international competition of Greek and foreign feature length films held annually in October in Thessaloniki.

"International Music Days"

Greek and foreign composers and musicians participate in these events organized annually by the International Fair of Thessaloniki sometime in April or May.

The open-air "Dasos" theatre

"Open Air Theatre Celebrations"

Performances by amateur-experimental Greek theatre groups organized annually by the Municipality of Thessaloniki during July and August.

"Children's Song Festival"

This event is organized annually by the Municipality of Kalamaria during the second half of September.

"The Gathering of Thessalonian Composers"

A local annual musical event organized by the Municipality of Kalamaria in the middle of September.

"The Chalkidiki Rally"

A European car rally organized annually by E.L.P.A. (Greek Automobile Association) in Chalkidiki at the end of August.

"The International Fair of Thessaloniki Rally"

An annual international rally organized by the Fair (HELEXPO) and the automobile club of Thessaloniki (ΟΑΘ) in September.

"International Tennis Tournament"

Organized by the Tennis Club of Thessaloniki every 15th of September.

"Ivanofeia"

Annual national swimming events organized by the Heracles Athletic Club sometime in October or November.

"Nautical Events"

"Koniordeia" sailing races in spring (Yachting Club of Thessaloniki)

"Velideia" sailing races in spring (Nautical Club of Kalamaria)

"Paraskevaidia" rowing races in mid-October (Nautical Club of Thessaloniki)

"Kornilakia" rowing races in June (Nautical Club of Kalamaria)

"Boukadoura" open sea races in August (Nautical Club of Thessaloniki)

"Air-Rally"

A contest of light single-engine planes in spring and

The "Hatziyiannaki Mills" in the area of the "Sfageia" district, now converted into an entertainment and exhibition area complex

autumn (Thessaloniki Flying Club)

"Wine Festival"

Held during the first two weeks of September and organized by the Touring Club, the Greek Tourist Authority, and the Municipality of Thessaloniki.

→
Aerial view of the city

Panoramic view of Thessaloniki

Thessaloniki: Sightseeing

Many sightseeing tours start from Thessaloniki, such as:

- *Ancient Pella,* capital of ancient Macedonia (40 kms from Thessaloniki on the way to Edessa.)
- *Vergina,* the site of the 4th century B.C. Macedonian tombs (near the village of Palatista, Veria)
- *Dion,* the holy site of the Macedonians (near Katerini, just 800 m from the village of Karitsa)
- Ancient *Olynthus,* the most important ancient city in Chalkidiki (between the villages Nea Moudania and Gerakini)
- The *Monastic State of Mt. Athos,* with its 20 monasteries, 14 cloisters, and other hermitages (foreign nationals require a visitor's permit obtained from the Alliens Dept. of the Ministry of Macedonia-Thrace)
- The *Petralona Cave* in Chalkidiki, where in 1960 the skull of the "archanthropos"

(archaic homo sapiens), at least 200,000 years old, was discovered among the stalagmites in the cave.

Other interesting places to visit are the lakes of Aghios Vasilios and Volvi (north of Thessaloniki), Mt. Olympus, the beaches around the gulf of Thermaikos, Chalkidiki, Pieria, and the gulf of Strymonikos.

Winter resorts worth visiting are *Seli* on Mt. Vermion (between Veria and Naousa), *Tria Pigadia* above Naousa, *Pisoderi* in Florina, *Lailias* in Serres, and the area of Olympus and Elassona. Thessaloniki has 58 hotels (a total of 3,926 rooms and 7,343 beds).

The Aristoteleio University of Thessaloniki

The University was founded in 1925 and is the largest institution of higher education in the country with 65,000 students (1992). It consists of nine schools, divided into 36 departments. These are the schools of:
— Theology
— Philosophy
— Applied Sciences
— Agriculture and Forestry
— Law and Economics
— Medicine
— Engineering
— Fine Arts, and
— Education.

The statue of Alexandros Papanastasiou on the university grounds

The University of Macedonia

An institute of higher education founded in Thessaloniki in 1990. Its aim is to serve the field of economics and social sciences. It is divided into five departments: economics, business administration and management, international and European economic studies, accounting and finance, applied information technology. It runs joint educational programmes with other European universities.

The University of Macedonia in Thessaloniki

The International Fair of Thessaloniki - HELEXPO

The International Fair of Thessaloniki was founded in 1925 and opened its gates to the public on 3 October 1926. Over 600 foreign and local exhibitors participated. Today the Fair is the focus of promotion on an international level for the multi-faceted Greek policy of friendship, commercial, and financial co-operation among nations.

Besides the main "Fair" in September, HELEXPO also organizes a number of specialized international exhibitions, such as:

AGROTICA: International exhibition of agricultural machinery, equipment, and supplies (January -February)

INFACOMA: International exhibition of construction material, heating, cooling, insulation, solar energy and technology (February)

PRODUCTS FROM CYPRUS: International exhibition of products from Cyprus to Greece (February - March)

The University of Thessaloniki swimming pool

FURNIDEC: International exhibition of furniture (March)

FURNIMA: International exhibition of machinery, raw materials, tools, equipment, and supplies for the production of furniture (March)

HYGEIA: International exhibition of medical, hospital, pharmaceutical, dental equipment, supplies and services (March)

MARMIN: International exhibition of marble-ores equipment and machinery (April)

GRAPHIS: International exhibition of stationary and school books (May)

THRACE: Greek trade exhibition in Komotini (May - June)

EPIRUS: Greek trade exhibition in Ioannina (June)

INFOSYSTEM: International exhibition of information systems and high technology products (October)

KOSMIMA: International exhibition of jewellery, watches, precious stones, machinery and equipment(October)

HOTELIA: International exhibition of supplies and equipment for

The International Fair of Thessaloniki

hotels, restaurants, confectionerey shops, bakeries, shops (October-November)

PHILOXENIA: International exhibition on Tourism (October - November)

Thessaloniki: Transportation

AIR: The "Macedonia Airport" of Thessaloniki provides facilities for domestic and international flights (Olympic Airways and other airlines). Domestic flight destinations include Athens, Heraclion, Rhodes, Mytilini, Ioannina, and Limnos. International flights include Frankfurt, Dusseldorf, Stuttgart, London, Paris, Bruxells, Copenhagen, Amsterdam, Vienna, and Zurich.

RAIL: An extensive rail network

The new Railway Station in Thessaloniki

connects Thessaloniki to Athens and with most main cities in the country as well as European capitals and cities in the Middle and Near East.

COACH SERVICES: Coaches operating from Thessaloniki give access to every city within Macedonia as well as the other main cities in the country.

The "Modiano" market place

The fish-market in Thessaloniki

USEFUL TELEPHONE NUMBERS

Emergency 166
First Aid -Red Cross
(Koundourioti - 22 Votsi st.) 530.530
First Aid - National Health (IKA) (Pyli Axiou)
(Polytechniou - 26 October st.) 522.585
Hospitals - Clinics 106
Pharmacies 107

Police 100
Fire Department 199
Port Authority 531.505
Military Police 837.500
Traffic Police
(4 Dodecannisou st.) 526.026
Police Directorate
(10 Egnatia - Tantalou st.) 522.821
Tourist Police 548.907
3rd Army Corps HQ 237.221
Automobile Association (ELPA) 104
Automobile Association
(Express Service) 154
M.O.T. 167

Greek Tourist Authority (EOT)
(34 Mitropoleos st.) 225.770
Hoteliers Association
of Thessaloniki 273.993
Tourist Information (EOT) 271.882
EOT Camping - Thermaikos   (0392) 51.360
EOT Camping - Asprovalta .   (0397) 31.249
EOT Camping - Epanomi . . .   (0392) 41.379
EOT Beach - Aghia Triada . .   (0392) 51.353
EOT Marina - Nea Krini 426.261

Telephone Enquiries . . . . 131 and 132
Post Office (Central) 277.434
Ministry of Macedonia - Thrace . . . 264.321
Prefecture of Thessaloniki 428.536
Municipality of Thessaloniki 238.321
Law Courts 522.021
Metropolis (Cathedral)
of Thessaloniki 228.823

University of Thessaloniki
(Rector's Office) 991.665
Port of Thessaloniki 526.221
International Fair of Thessaloniki -
HELEXPO
(154 Egnatia st.) 239.221
Archaeological Museum 830.538
Museum of the
Macedonian Struggle 229.778
Folk Life and
Ethonological Museum 830.591
State Theatre 223.785
Railway Station 517.517/8

AIRLINES
Austrian Airlines (1 L. Nikis st.) . . . 239.421
British Airways
(4 Ionos Dragoumi st.) 242.005
Cyprus Airways
(12 Komninon st.) 228.352
Goldair Ltd. Athenair Ltd
(20 Kalapothaki st.) 236.454
(Local Representatives for:
Biman, CSA, LOT, MALEV, PIA, LAP,
Philippine Airlines, Zambia Airways)
Lufthansa (31 L. Nikis st.) 235.722
Olympic Airways
(3 Koundourioti st.) 260.122
Swissair (1 L. Nikis st.) 267.552

BANKS:
Bank of Greece 538.320
National Bank of Greece 538.621
KTIMATIKI Bank 262.532
Commercial Bank 532.221
Ionian Bank 270.540
Bank of Macedonia - Thrace 542.213
Credit Bank 229.058
Bank of Crete 262.988
Stegastiki Bank 287.312
E.T.B.A. 275.101
Agricultural Bank 271.262
Xios Bank 241.896

American Express 261.521
The Chase Manhattan Bank 236.221
Credit Commercial de France 533.454
Citibank 266.021
National Westminster Bank 531.007
The Bank of Nova Scotia 236.131

CAR RENTALS
Avis Rent-a-Car 227.126
Hertz 224.906
AutoRent 811.880
Interrent 826.333
Hellas Cars LTD 223.927
Salonica 277.015

CONSULATES
Austrian (81 Egnatia st.) 228.184
Belgian (8 Dodecannisou st.) 538.157
Bulgarian (12 Nik. Manou st.) 829.210
French (8 M. King st.) 244.030
German (4a Charles Diehl st.) 236.315

Yugoslavian (4 Komninon st.) 244.265
Danish (26 Komninon st.) 284.065
Swiss (55 L. Nikis st.) 234.442
USA (59 L. Nikis st.) 242.905
Spanish (9 V. Hugo st.) 515.391
Italian (1 Fleming st.) 830.055
Cypriot (37 L. Nikis st.) 260.611
British (8 Venizelou st.) 278.006
Mexican (311 Monasteriou st.) 526.397
Norwegian
(17 Pringipos Nikolaou st.) 270.666
Southafrican Union 697.594
Dutch (25 Komninon st.) 284.065
Hungarian (63 Egnatias st.) 221.442
Peruvian
(Tsimiski - 18 Charles Diehl st.) . . . 229.377
Portuguese (3 L. Nikis st.) 228.138
Swedish (26 Komninon st.) 227.477
Turkish (151 Ag. Demetriou st.) . . . 248.452
Finnish (4 I. Dragoumi st.) 278.840
Chilean (24 Kolokotroni st.) 656.041

Casa Bianca in Thessaloniki prior to its restoration

A part of Byzantine Walls of Acropolis

Exterior Gate

Trigonion of Alysos Tower

St. Demetrius Hospital (Dimotico)

Anna Paleologina Gate

The Eptapirgion

St. Nikolaos Orphano's Church

Acropolis

St. Taxiarchas Church

The Walls

KASTROU

AGIOU PAVLOU

St. Laodigitria Church

Eski-Delik Gate

The Walls

Vlatades Monastery

Hosios David Church

KOZANIS

Alatza Imaret

St. Demetrios Church

"The Fortune" of Thessaloniki

Emmanuel Tower

Prophet Elias

Yeni Hamam

Roman Agora

St. Demetrios (Mosaic from his Church)

Yeni Delik Gate

Turbe

Diikitirio

St. Katerina

AGIOU DIMITRIOU

St. Apostoli Church

Letaia Gate (Yeni Kapou)

Cistern

94

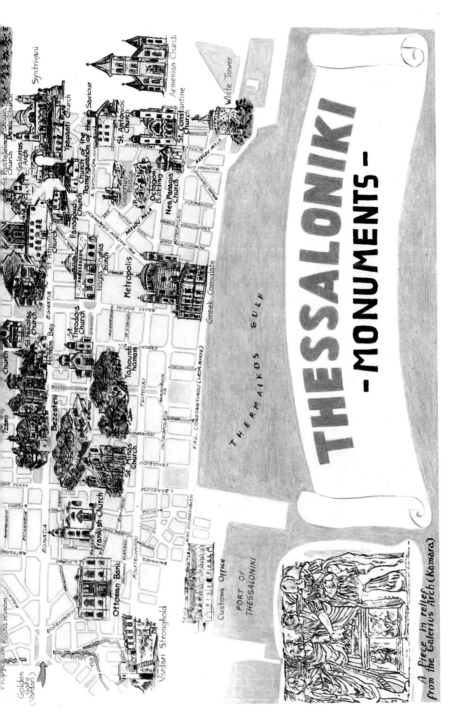

THESSALONIKI
– MONUMENTS –

A Piece in relief from the Galerius Arch (Kamara)

PORT OF THESSALONIKI

Customs Office

THERMAIKOS GULF

Greek Consulate

White Tower

Contents